LET US
GIVE

LET US GIVE

Scriptural Reflections for

Introducing Offerings

Arthur E. Ball

Kregel
Publications

Let Us Give: Scriptural Reflections for Introducing Offerings

© 2003 by Arthur E. Ball

Published by Kregel Publications, P.O. Box 2607, Grand Rapids, MI 49501.

Library of Congress Cataloging-in-Publication Data
Ball, Arthur E.
Let us give: Scriptural reflections for introducing offerings / by Arthur E. Ball.
    p. cm.
Includes index.
    1. Stewardship, Christian—Biblical teaching. 2. Christian giving—Biblical teaching. 3. Bible—Criticism, interpretation, etc. I. Title.
BS680.S78B35   2003
248.6—dc21   2003009056

ISBN 0-8254-2084-9

Printed in the United States of America

03 04 05 06 07 / 5 4 3 2 1

Dedicated to
my pastor,
Dr. James Dennis,
a doer of the Word,
not just a hearer.

Contents

Introduction

THE PURPOSE OF THIS BOOK is to address the often-touchy subject of giving to God—or stewardship, as some prefer to call it. As you read, you will notice that many of the verses highlighted in this work do not refer directly to money or giving. Fear not. God does not always instruct us by direct remark (although it is certainly one way in which He communicates). Sometimes the lesson is found in a principle, or in the details of biographical sketch, such as the story of the life of David. Regardless of which of these three ways—direct remark, principle, or biographical sketch—God chooses as His means of instruction, the lesson is the same. He wants us to give—freely, cheerfully, and generously—to His service.

I hope that God's Word will address your heart and your purse in relation to the vital matter of Christian stewardship in the local church. After all, if we don't give and support God's work as our Lord intended, who will?

In a time when so many in the church are focused on the fruits of the Spirit and finding their "gifts," may we "abound in this grace also" in our Lord Jesus Christ—the grace of giving (2 Corinthians 8:7).

LET US
GIVE

Giving from the Heart

Luke 6:38

> *Give, and it shall be given unto you; good measure, pressed down, and shaken together, and running over, shall men give into your bosom. For with the same measure that ye mete withal it shall be measured to you again.*

WHAT DOES A RIGHTEOUS MAN or woman look like? How can we distinguish a righteous one from all the others? In the Sermon on the Mount, very early in His earthly ministry, Jesus gave a masterful explanation of the characteristics that distinguish a truly righteous person—one who is indeed "right with God."

One of the hallmarks of righteousness that Jesus mentioned is a willingness to *give* generously. He said the righteous will be blessed in direct proportion to the measure or standard by which they give. If people are reluctant and self-serving in their giving, God will be reluctant and conservative with any blessings He allows to return to the giver. Think about that!

The truly righteous give not because it is a stern requirement. They give because their righteousness has infected them with a generous heart.

We don't give because we have to—we give because we want to.

Let us give as the righteous give—those who are right with God.

You Don't Get to Keep It

Matthew 10:8

> *Heal the sick, cleanse the lepers, raise the dead, cast out devils:*
> *freely ye have received, freely give.*

WHEN JESUS COMMISSIONED His disciples to go out and preach to the lost sheep of the house of Israel, announcing that the kingdom of heaven was at hand, He did not expect them to work in a powerless vacuum. Instead, He equipped them with power to heal the sick, cast out devils, and even raise the dead. He gave them every asset they would need, and supplied them abundantly. Then He cautioned them with these words: "Freely ye have received, freely give."

Fellow Christian, can you name anything you own that was not given to you by God? Even our ability to accumulate wealth is a gift from God. Wise believers understand that everything we own is only borrowed for the short season of our earthly lives. As Solomon writes in Ecclesiastes, it will all be left behind for others who will follow.

When we understand the principle of who really owns our possessions—God—it takes the struggle out of giving generously. Because we have received freely, we can give freely.

Let us give freely—as those who have freely received.

The Greatest Offering

Hebrews 10:10

By the which will we are sanctified through the offering of the body of Jesus Christ once for all.

OUR LORD JESUS CHRIST, in offering Himself on Calvary, gave the greatest offering ever presented. Heaven's best, dying on behalf of earth's fallen race of sinners. He alone was the perfect offering—the only offering acceptable to a holy God as atonement for our sins. His offering was perfect in its accomplishment, because it set apart, or sanctified, every believer once and for all. As a result of Christ's sacrifice, we've been set apart to receive forgiveness *from* God, enjoy fellowship *with* God, and offer service *to* God.

Our money in the offering plate at church does not save us. Whether or not we even give an offering does not save us. However, the fact that Christ offered Himself—perfect and sinless—to atone for our sins raises an important question for the genuine believer.

If we realize that we have been purchased from the penalty and power of sin by the Savior's perfect offering, how can we live in the light of such knowledge without having a keen desire to give offerings of our own in the service of our Savior?

Those who understand that they have been purchased by the greatest offering—the Lord Jesus Christ Himself—will have no reservations about offering to Him their own body and material possessions.

Let us give an offering as those who have been purchased for eternity by the Lord Jesus Christ Himself.

Giving with God Looking over Our Shoulder

Acts 8:18–20

> *And when Simon saw that through laying on of the apostles' hands the Holy Ghost was given, he offered them money, saying, Give me also this power, that on whomsoever I lay hands, he may receive the Holy Ghost. But Peter said unto him, Thy money perish with thee, because thou hast thought that the gift of God may be purchased with money.*

SIMON THE SORCERER WANTED to give his money for something in the Lord's work. But it was money offered with the wrong motive and in the wrong way.

Simon was willing to give because he thought he would get back something that would bring him prestige, popularity, and power. None of these motives is a good reason to give an offering to the Lord Jesus Christ.

Simon also gave in the wrong way because he did not give his alms in secret, as our Lord had taught earlier. It was also not a freewill offering. He was giving money with an expectation that he would receive something substantial in return.

Christians who want to please the Lord will give with a proper motive and in the right way. Other people may look at our outward performance, but God looks at our hearts.

Let us give freely and out of a full heart, expecting no gain for our own ends, knowing that God is looking over our shoulder.

The Offering: Delightful or Despised?

Psalm 40:8

> *I delight to do thy will, O my God: yea, thy law is within my heart.*

DOING THE WILL OF GOD and delighting in it are not necessarily the same thing. A child who hates vegetables may eat them to the very last bite when they are served to him, but that does not mean he takes delight in doing the will of his parents.

It is God's will for believers that we give offerings. But whether we delight in fulfilling this part of God's will may be another thing entirely.

We are called to love the Lord our God with all of our heart, all of our soul, and all of our mind. But do we take genuine delight in bringing our offerings? Or is the offering time a sort of "necessary nuisance," a hurdle to be dutifully bounded over so we can get on with the real worship?

If we find ourselves struggling with the idea of giving an offering, if we are offended when money is mentioned from the pulpit, perhaps we are not delighting ourselves in the Lord in every way that we should.

How do we genuinely feel about the offering time in our church? Genuine relief when it is over, or genuine joy at the privilege of participation?

How delighted the Lord is with a delighted giver.

Let us give as those who delight in every aspect of His service.

Is Tithing Dead in the New Testament?

Deuteronomy 14:22–23

> *Thou shalt truly tithe all the increase of thy seed, that the field bringeth forth year by year. And thou shalt eat before the Lord thy God, in the place which he shall choose to place his name there, the tithe of thy corn, of thy wine, and of thine oil, and the firstlings of thy herds and of thy flocks; that thou mayest learn to fear the Lord thy God always.*

THE IDEA THAT TITHING IS only a relic of the Old Testament Mosaic law is enticing. After all, are we not living in the New Testament age of grace? Have we not been freed from bondage to the Old Testament law?

The New Testament believer is indeed free from bondage to the Old Testament law, but we are not free from the principle of it. Why would we want to be?

The principle of tithing in the Old Testament is a clear signal that our giving, in God's mind, should be deliberate, systematic, proportional, regular, and generous.

Bear in mind that tithing is not something that appeared on the scene only when the law came. It was practiced long before the law when Abram gave a tithe of all he possessed to Melchizedek—a foreshadowing of Christ, who was yet to come.

How could we, as New Testament believers living under grace, actually consider giving less in our offerings than those who were under the constraints of the law? As New Testament believers, our giving really only begins after we have tithed to our local church.

Let us give, not as those who are under bondage to the law, but as those who are free to give all under grace.

Giving: For My House or God's House?

Nehemiah 10:39

> *For the children of Israel and the children of Levi shall bring the offering of the corn, of the new wine, and the oil, unto the chambers, where are the vessels of the sanctuary, and the priests that minister, and the porters, and the singers: and we will not forsake the house of our God.*

"WE WILL NOT FORSAKE THE house of our God" aptly summarizes the philosophy of every honest believer, whether in the Old Testament age of the law or the New Testament era of grace.

In our present generation, we understand clearly the need to make payments religiously on mortgage loans, credit cards, automobile installments, and a host of other financial obligations into which we have eagerly entered. Yet, how often is the house of God abandoned financially because "there just isn't enough money" on hand to give anything substantial to the Lord's work?

The believer understands the importance, even the necessity, of tending to the house of God with material offerings. May we write these letters large at the top of our personal budgets: "We will not forsake the house of our God."

Let us give with a heart that refuses to forsake the house of our God, no matter what the other circumstances of life may be.

God Is Interested in *How* You Give

Psalm 51:16–17

> *For thou desirest not sacrifice; else would I give it: thou delightest not in burnt offering. The sacrifices of God are a broken spirit: a broken and a contrite heart, O God, thou wilt not despise.*

THIS PSALM IS DAVID'S magnificent plea of repentance after he sinned with Bathsheba and murdered her husband. It is a masterpiece of supplication to a Holy God from the mouth and heart of a genuine penitent.

David understood all too clearly that the act of making offerings alone is not what captures the attention of God. Instead, it is the state of genuine humility and true repentance in the heart of the one making the offering that draws the recognition of God.

Whether we are able to give much or little, it is the motive of our heart in making the offering that stirs the heart of God.

Giving isn't always about how *much* we give, but it is always about *how* we give. "A broken and a contrite heart, O God, thou wilt not despise."

Let us give whatever we give with a genuine affection for God and for pleasing Him.

"I'll Give Later, When I Can Afford It"

Proverbs 22:9

> *He that hath a bountiful eye shall be blessed; for he giveth of his bread to the poor.*

THE VERSE DOES NOT SAY, He that hath a bountiful *purse* shall be blessed; it says, He that hath a bountiful *eye* shall be blessed. Jesus rejoiced in the minimal offering given by the poor widow, because she gave all that she possessed. She did not have a bountiful purse, but she did have a bountiful eye.

Many of us live our lives, year after year, telling ourselves that we will give more "someday" when we have more to give. With such an outlook, however, the ugly truth is that the golden day never arrives when we actually have "enough" to give a bountiful offering. Why? Because we do not have a bountiful eye.

We are not accountable to God *today* for the bounty we may possibly possess tomorrow—or *someday*. We are, however, accountable to God today for whatever we presently possess, and for whether or not we are stewards with a bountiful eye, who give of our "bread" for His honor and praise.

Let us give as those who have a tender heart and a bountiful eye toward the work of God and His church.

26

Stingy Offerings to a Generous God

Psalm 13:6

> *I will sing unto the Lord, because he hath dealt bountifully with me.*

A CHRISTIAN WOMAN WHO attended a certain church was asked to give a testimony about the blessings and goodness of God in her life. She thought for a moment and then asked to be excused from the assignment, because she could not think of anything to say. Later, she repented when she realized just how bountifully, how generously, and how wonderfully God had dealt with her over the years. Had He not saved her from sin and the terrible penalty of sin? Had He not blessed her with more good days than bad ones? Had He not been patient with her in her slowness to grow in the grace of Christ?

But this woman is not the only one with whom God has dealt bountifully. He blesses every believer. The unsaved never quite realize this truth, whereas believers become more keenly aware of it as they grow in the grace and knowledge of the Lord Jesus Christ.

Has God not dealt bountifully with us? How is it, then, that we can be stingy with our offerings to God?

The believer's measure for giving should never be, "How little can I get away with giving?" Rather, we should ask ourselves, "What is the *most* I can do?"

Let us give bountifully to our God, who has dealt so bountifully with us.

God Won't Be Bought with Our Gifts

Matthew 5:21–24

> *Ye have heard that it was said by them of old time, Thou shalt not kill; and whosoever shall kill shall be in danger of the judgment: But I say unto you, That whosoever is angry with his brother without a cause shall be in danger of the judgment: and whosoever shall say to his brother, Raca, shall be in danger of the council: but whosoever shall say, Thou fool, shall be in danger of hell fire. Therefore if thou bring thy gift to the altar, and there rememberest that thy brother hath ought against thee; Leave there thy gift before the altar, and go thy way; first be reconciled to thy brother, and then come and offer thy gift.*

THE GIVING OF AN OFFERING to God should always be a good thing. Good for the one who gives, and certainly good for the work of God. But it seems that Jesus put a qualification on the matter of giving offerings.

The sin of an unrepaired relationship with a brother or sister in Christ is not excused because we bring an offering to God. He will not be bought off with our presents.

If we take seriously the words of our Lord Jesus Christ here, the offering time becomes something more than a distracting exercise in the order of worship. It becomes a time of self-examination. Is my heart right with God? Are my relationships with my brothers and sisters in Christ in their right order? Is there unjustified anger in my heart? Am I nursing a grudge?

Notice that Jesus did not excuse the sinful giver from his giving. He only directed him to delay his giving until his relationships were put in order. Then, and only then, would the offering be acceptable.

Our giving never purchases favor with God. But when our heart is in full favor with God and with our brethren in Christ, we are then eligible for the privilege and blessing of giving.

Let us give, having examined our hearts and our relationships with others, so that our offering will be acceptable in His sight.

"But I Gave Last Week!"

Hebrews 9:25–26

Nor yet that he should offer himself often, as the high priest entereth into the holy place every year with blood of others; for then must he often have suffered since the foundation of the world: but now once in the end of the world hath he appeared to put away sin by the sacrifice of himself.

IT IS AN ACCEPTED FACT THAT Jesus needed to die on the cross only once. He was the final fulfillment of all the sacrificial sin offerings of the Old Testament. In Him alone we find the sufficient offering for the forgiveness of our sins. Once and for all time.

The life of the believer, who has been washed from sin by the final and all-fulfilling offering of the Lord Jesus Christ, should be a continual offering of praise, sacrifice, and giving.

Instead of looking upon each Sunday as a separate offering, we should look upon our lives as one continual offering. Each Sunday should simply be an installment in our continual offering of praise, service, and giving.

When we realize this great truth, we are spared from the "But, I gave last week!" mentality that hobbles so many Christians.

Let us give as those who understand the offering as a continual, lifelong joy and privilege.

Charity's Better-Known Sister

1 Corinthians 13:3

> *And though I bestow all my goods to feed the poor, and though I give my body to be burned, and have not charity, it profiteth me nothing.*

CHARITY'S BETTER-KNOWN SISTER—often mistakenly called "charity" herself—is alive and well today in the form of many worthwhile causes. These causes raise money for their needs in a variety of ways. The general public is usually more than glad to enter into these fund-raising efforts for "a worthy cause."

The true identity of charity, the lesser-known sister, is not these worthy causes, but rather a state of mind, an attitude of heart. Real charity is actually a spiritual grace of Christ that resides in the heart of true believers. She is easy to recognize—being amply described in 1 Corinthians 13—but has been hidden for years behind her better-known sister. The fact that many churches have been forced to register as "charities" has further obscured the lesser-known yet genuine sister known as charity.

Giving an offering to God's work does not necessarily make us charitable by the standard of biblical charity. We are not to give to the church as if it were a charity. We are to give to God's work with a heart that is governed by biblical charity—a charity that touches every part of our lives.

Let us not just give offerings to charity; let us give our offerings out of a heart of charity.

The Three Calls of God Urging Us to Give

Psalm 29:1–2

Give unto the Lord, O ye mighty, give unto the Lord glory and strength. Give unto the Lord the glory due unto his name; worship the Lord in the beauty of holiness.

THREE CALLS TO GIVE RING out from these verses.

The first call is to the mighty. According to Peter, the believer is not mighty within himself, but is to humble himself under the mighty hand of God that he may be exalted in due time. Mighty men in waiting.

The second call challenges us to give God the proper place in our lives that recognizes His glory and strength.

The third call instructs us to ascribe the proper glory to His name, giving all to Him that we should.

After these three calls have been met—then, and only then can we come to the lofty subject of worship.

There are many voices in our generation calling upon us to give for one purpose or another. But we should be sensitive, first and foremost, to the calls of God upon our lives to give so that we may enter into real worship.

Many would say they don't like to talk about giving in church, but God does.

Let us give because we understand it to be a calling of the voice of God.

Daring to Give as Jesus Gave

Mark 15:22–23

> *And they bring him unto the place Golgotha, which is, being interpreted, The place of a skull. And they gave him to drink wine mingled with myrrh: but he received it not.*

THESE ARE NOT PLEASANT verses to look at. Our Lord Jesus Christ is in the abyss of suffering, through which He must pass in order to purchase our redemption from sin and eternal torment.

It is during one of those anguishing moments that our Savior is offered some wine mingled with myrrh. The nails are yet to be driven into His hands and feet. The agony of being suspended upon a cross still awaits Him with greedy misery. No one would have blamed Jesus for accepting something to dull the senses when they were under such brutal assault. We almost hope He will accept this little assuagement, pitifully insufficient as it is. But He does not. His offering for our sins will not be blemished by even the slightest exception. He will feel, suffer, and bear every pain of our judgment. He will drink the bitter cup that the Father has set before Him. Every drop. He will give everything. He will hold back nothing.

Do we give in like manner? Or are we looking for a more convenient and painless way?

We cannot give what Jesus gave, but we can give as Jesus gave. Dare we?

Let us intentionally and joyously give in the same mind with which Jesus gave.

God Is Not a Beggar

Luke 24:41–43

> *And while they yet believed not for joy, and wondered, he said unto them, Have ye here any meat? And they gave him a piece of broiled fish, and of an honeycomb. And he took it, and did eat before them.*

THE LORD JESUS, RISEN FROM the dead and in His glorious body, stands before His wondering disciples. He has tasted death for every man, now He tastes a honeycomb.

When Jesus asks the men, "Have ye here any meat?" it is not the question of a beggar; rather, it is the question of a great teacher.

Jesus actually needed nothing from these men. Nothing. But to instruct and edify them, He asks for something to eat. His purpose was to teach them two important lessons.

First, they would learn that the risen Jesus is not a ghost or a spirit. He is real—flesh and bones. Our Savior is not a phantom.

Second, they would be invited to contribute something of their own stores as evidence of His reality and of the reality of their faith.

When as New Testament believers we give an offering through the local church, we accomplish the same twofold purpose. We give evidence of the reality of our faith and in the reality of the Lord Jesus Christ and His ongoing work beyond the tomb. He asks for an offering, not because He is a beggar, but because it bolsters our faith!

Let us give—as evidence of the reality of our faith in the reality of the living Savior.

An Empty Vine

Hosea 10:1

> *Israel is an empty vine, he bringeth forth fruit unto himself:*
> *according to the multitude of his fruit he hath increased the*
> *altars; according to the goodness of his land they have made*
> *goodly images.*

THE FIRST FIVE WORDS OF THIS verse are ones that no believer should ever wish to hear from the Savior. May the day never come that our Lord Jesus Christ would say such a thing about us.

Fruitless vines must be pruned—or, even worse, cut down and thrown into the fire. What an unimaginable thought for a nation or an individual, to be declared an empty vine.

There are many fruits in the Christian life. Giving offerings is certainly one of those fruits. When we give an offering through our local church, we give something back to God just as surely as the vine gives its fruit back to the vinedresser.

When our Lord looks upon us, does He pronounce us fruitless or does He rejoice at the harvest we bring forth for His praise?

Fruitfulness in giving is an evidence of the life and health of the vine.

Let us give so that our Lord may declare us to be fruitful vines.

The Lord Remember All Your Offerings

Psalm 20:1–3

> *The Lord hear thee in the day of trouble; the name of the God of Jacob defend thee; send thee help from the sanctuary, and strengthen thee out of Zion; remember all thy offerings, and accept thy burnt sacrifice; Selah.*

THIS PASSAGE REFERS TO various offerings given under the Old Testament system. But the psalmist, David, reminds us of a privilege that follows those who have given offerings to God. As he puts it in one of his more famous psalms: "Goodness and mercy shall follow me all the days of my life" (Psalm 23:6).

The day of trouble comes to every believer. When it does, we cry out to God for strength, comfort, victory, or all three. In the day of trouble, it is a good thing to be able to come to God as one who has faithfully lived "the offering life." Reminding God of our faithfulness in giving is an important prayer instrument—and it energizes our prayers for other believers who are in need.

Make no mistake. We are not talking about purchasing God's favor. We are talking about coming to God with the evidence of our faith. James writes, "Shew me thy faith without thy works, and I will shew thee my faith by my works" (James 2:18).

It is good to be able to show God our faith by our works. Especially in the day of trouble. As the psalmist says, "The LORD hear thee in the day of trouble; . . . remember all thy offerings, . . . Selah." Think about that.

Let us give unconditionally, understanding the confidence in prayer that it may afford us in the day of trouble.

When God Audits the Believer's Books

Luke 12:48

> *But he that knew not, and did commit things worthy of stripes, shall be beaten with few stripes. For unto whomsoever much is given, of him shall be much required: and to whom men have committed much, of him they will ask the more.*

AT THE END OF HIS PARABLE about the importance of being a watchful servant, Jesus closes with the observation that much is required of those who have been entrusted with much.

We might be tempted to turn away from this passage, thinking that it doesn't apply to us who seem to have so little. Consider this: The standard that Jesus establishes here is proportional. We may have little, but we are nonetheless required to be faithful with what we have. The lesson here is not just for the rich. It is for every believer in every income bracket. We are accountable to God in proportion to what He has entrusted to us.

Audit day is coming. How will we fare when the accounts of our stewardship are settled before God?

Let us give as those who understand that our Lord will indeed audit our books one day, whether we have much or little.

The Mistake of the Easy Offering

John 19:30

> *When Jesus therefore had received the vinegar, he said, It is finished: and he bowed his head, and gave up the ghost.*

CALVARY WOULD HAVE MEANT nothing had Jesus not presented Himself as the perfect offering—sinless, without blemish or fault, both physically and spiritually.

At Calvary, as at every place along the way, Jesus did everything required of Him by His heavenly Father. Consequently, He was the only acceptable offering for our sins. It cost our Lord Jesus Christ more than we will ever know this side of heaven.

It is understood that believers are neither saved nor kept by the offerings they make. But there is still a truth in one of the principles found in Jesus' offering. Our offerings should be complete and sacrificial.

Giving a partial offering of leftovers, or a non-sacrificial offering through some fund-raising scheme, is not the sacrificial offering that Jesus modeled for us.

Calvary would have meant nothing if Jesus had not given sacrificially and given everything. Likewise, an offering that is easy—one that costs us nothing or comes from something we will never miss anyway—probably isn't a real offering, when all is said and done.

---

*Let us give as those who would salute their Sovereign
and not be wearied by the cost.*

A Measure for the Believer's Giving

Psalm 68:19

> *Blessed be the Lord, who daily loadeth us with benefits, even the God of our salvation. Selah.*

THIS VERSE IS NOT DIVINE hyperbole. We really should bless, thank, praise, and serve the Lord in the knowledge that He really does load us daily with benefits.

Is not life itself a benefit? Have we not had more good days in our lives than bad ones? How many simple blessings do we take for granted each day? Do we consider the companionship of someone we love—our family and close friends? What about our local church? Our pastor? What about something as simple as the taste of fresh water when we are thirsty, or the flavor of a favorite food? How about a refreshing night's sleep? The list goes on and on. Have we ever really noticed?

Even the unsaved enjoy most of the benefits we could name. But it is in the hearts of Christians that the magnitude of God's blessing is fully appreciated. As Christians, our eyes are opened to a veritable flood of blessings overflowing from the hand of God.

He has loaded us *daily* with many benefits. Now, how shall we give back to Him? Shall we throw Him a few scraps of whatever is most convenient for us? Shall we play the game of "how little can I get away with?" when it comes to giving through His church? Sincere Christians realize that these ways of thinking will never do. God must have our best, our most, our first. May we never be embarrassed before God someday because we are shown to have spent more on our pets, our hobbies, and our pastimes than we invested in our offerings and service to Him.

Let us give as those who are so wonderfully and thankfully aware of all that God has given to us.

A Double Danger

Luke 12:15

> *And he said unto them, Take heed, and beware of covetousness:*
> *for a man's life consisteth not in the abundance of the things*
> *which he possesseth.*

WHEN OUR LORD JESUS CHRIST issues a double warning, "take heed and beware," He wants us to know about something dangerous.

First, He would have us avoid covetousness—a reminder of the tenth commandment given to Moses (the last commandment and one of the least heeded). Jesus knew that most other sins are bound up in the sin of coveting what is not ours. He says, "Take heed. Beware."

Next, Jesus exposes the false notion that our quality of life will increase in direct proportion to the amount of wealth or things that we possess. We may laugh at the bumper sticker that says, "He who dies with the most toys wins," but far too many people actually live their lives according to that malignant philosophy. Too bad they can't be interviewed on the subject *after* they've had a glimpse of eternity.

The "dangerous duo" mentioned here by our Lord Jesus— covetousness and the mistaken idea that accumulating possessions will increase our happiness—are probably two of the greatest enemies of biblical, joyous giving.

Our Savior posted a double warning sign at this treacherous point along the road of life so we will not fall into the ditch. We see the danger. Let's stay well clear of it.

Let us give as those who are aware of the "dangerous duo" and have
determined not to be overcome by them.

Giving to a Cause That Cannot Fail

Psalm 138:2

> *I will worship toward thy holy temple, and praise thy name for thy lovingkindness and for thy truth: for thou hast magnified thy word above all thy name.*

THE PSALMIST DOES NOT SAY that the Lord *hopes* to magnify His Word. He has already done it! He is not a struggling, well-meaning, yet inept God who someday hopes to be successful. He already is successful. He is sovereign!

We don't offer our worship and praise to God in the hopes that He might one day succeed. He has already succeeded. He is simply in the process of carrying out His divine will, His divine plan. He cannot fail. He will succeed with or without us.

How can we worship and praise such a great and accomplished God and not have a generous spirit toward Him in our giving? It would be a complete contradiction for us to withhold anything from God. If He cannot fail—and He cannot—why would we want to do anything less than abandon ourselves to His service at every level?

Giving is not the only way to worship God, but it would be nearly impossible to worship and praise Him without giving the full measure that we should.

Let us give as those who would worship and praise the God who cannot fail.

The First Emotion of the Redeemed Soul

Romans 1:20–21

> *For the invisible things of him from the creation of the world are clearly seen, being understood by the things that are made, even his eternal power and Godhead; so that they are without excuse: because that, when they knew God, they glorified him not as God, neither were thankful; but became vain in their imaginations, and their foolish heart was darkened.*

AN UNTHANKFUL HEART IS THE controlling influence of an unredeemed life. Atheists curse God with the very breath they have so graciously been granted from the very God they refuse to acknowledge. Worldlings greedily descend into the madness of moral sin without ever realizing that the very health with which they enjoy their sinful adventures has been granted to them from on high. Thankfulness to God is something that does not occur naturally to lost sinners, no matter how moral or respectable they may appear. Listen to their words: "I am self-made," one will say. "I am where I am today because I have worked hard and made something of myself," declares another. The thought of thanking God for His grace and His mercy never darkens even a corner of their minds.

However, a wonderful thing happens when a newly redeemed soul first awakens in the day of their salvation. Thankfulness—gratitude— springs forth in all its glory and promptly begins to distinguish the life of the new believer. It may take a period of growth in the grace and knowledge of the Lord Jesus Christ for someone to learn all the ways that thankfulness can be expressed, but gratitude has come to stay and begins planting her beautiful flowers throughout the heart of the believer.

The truly redeemed soul does not have a weekly wrestling match with doubt about whether or not to give an offering. The thankful, redeemed heart has only one question: What is the *most* I can do?

Let us give our offerings out of gratitude and thankfulness.

Selfishness Is Banished by Giving

Philippians 2:4

> *Look not every man on his own things, but every man also on the things of others.*

Selfishness IS LIVING AND MAKING life decisions as if there were no one else in the world. Whether it's as simple as taking up two or three spaces in a parking lot, or as complicated as a cheating husband who wrecks his own home—and someone else's—for an hour of sinful pleasure, selfish living can be hazardous to your health.

Our text speaks of "the things of others." It is "the things of others" that motivate the missionary, the soul-winning evangelist, the pastor, and the faithful church worker. In the life of a believer, selfish intentions and desires are trampled under in the stampede to respond to "the things of others."

Giving also has to do with "the things of others." As born-again, baptized believers, we understand that our income is given to us for purposes of stewardship. In our stewardship, we must consider "the things of others," the gospel work around the world, as we determine how to utilize the things we possess. They have not been given to us simply for our personal pleasure and whims, but to fulfill the higher purposes of God.

Let us give in the spirit of our Lord Jesus Christ, who was so tender to "the things of others."

A Holy Abandonment in Our Giving

1 Kings 8:5

> *And king Solomon, and all the congregation of Israel, that were assembled unto him, were with him before the ark, sacrificing sheep and oxen, that could not be told nor numbered for multitude.*

THERE IS AN UNSPOKEN, unwritten fear among many in the church that they might do too much—might become carried away—in their giving. They carefully regulate their gifts, lest their generosity get out of hand.

There is something wrong with such a mind-set. Solomon and the congregation of Israel would not have understood such thinking. They might be amazed at the grudging attitude of our generation of believers when it comes to the subject of giving.

Solomon and the people sacrificed material possessions "that could not be told nor numbered for multitude." Under Moses, the people gave so generously in their offerings for the tabernacle that word had to be sent for the people to stop giving, because they had actually given too much (Exodus 36:4–7). When was the last time a New Testament church fit either of these descriptions?

We abandon ourselves to financial commitments for so many things in life—mostly things for ourselves. Should we not abandon ourselves to giving for the greatest work in the world? Should we not give so generously to the work of our Lord Jesus Christ, through His local church, that it could not be told or numbered? Think what could be accomplished!

Let us give as those who have abandoned themselves to God.

No Struggle in Our Giving

Isaiah 11:5

> *And righteousness shall be the girdle of his loins, and faithfulness the girdle of his reins.*

THE PERSON AND GOVERNMENT of our Lord Jesus Christ during His millennial reign are described in Isaiah 11—perfect government, perfect order. There is an agreement of all the elements and inhabitants of the earth—mankind and beast, nature and creature. There has been nothing like it on earth since the earliest days of the Garden of Eden.

Perfect order does not yet exist, of course, but one day it will. Until then, we must live in a world characterized by disorder in societies, laws, religious observances, and general conduct. The believer whispers daily, "Come quickly Lord Jesus."

Amid our present circumstances, believers are being prepared for a better world yet to come—the perfect government of our Lord Jesus Christ. At the moment of salvation, the divine apparatus of cooperation and harmony was placed in our hearts—and we must use it even now.

In full cooperation with the divine government of the Lord Jesus Christ, believers have entered into an agreement to offer up every service and offering possible. For the time being, until Christ returns, the seat of His government can be found in the local church.

When we recognize that our Lord and King has chosen to express His government visibly through the local church, we will not struggle or have a conflict with helping to meet the material needs of the local church. Through our generous offerings, we fill the King's treasury.

Let us give as those who are in harmony with our Lord's government, not as those who are in conflict with it.

Faithfully Doing Our Part

Psalm 2:8

> *Ask of me, and I will give thee the heathen for thine inheritance, and the uttermost parts of the earth for thy possession.*

THE LORD JESUS CHRIST IS the head of the church. He is the ruler of all things. By divine decree, He lacks nothing. Yet, it is a common assumption, when it comes time to give an offering to the church, that we are somehow helping a Savior who needs our assistance lest He should fail.

How different things would look if we were to view life from His perspective. He is Owner, Master, and Lord of all things, and He calls upon His servants to faithfully do their part out of what He has given them.

Let's not flatter ourselves by imagining we are giving "poor Jesus" a helping hand. Let us rather view our giving as proof of our faithfulness, love, and productivity in Him. Let our giving stand as proof that we have gladly entered into His great plan for our lives through the local church, each believer faithfully doing his or her part for the honor and glory of Jesus Christ.

Let us give as those who are living proof that we are part of Christ's living church, doing our part.

Does Money Really Talk?

2 Corinthians 8:21

Providing for honest things, not only in the sight of the Lord, but also in the sight of men.

THE SCRIPTURES GIVE US AN impressive array of reasons for faithful and generous giving in the service of our Lord Jesus Christ through His local church. This verse touches upon one of the more practical ones. Simply put, we are to give so that the Lord's work will have an honest testimony in a community of unsaved people. At an even more basic level, we give so that the church can pay its bills on time and not end up with a defective reputation. The work of our Lord Jesus Christ would suffer reproach if business dealings were handled poorly and bills were not paid on time. Some would love to have such stones to throw at the church.

Money given through the local church sends a clear message to the unsaved community by preserving the church's financial integrity. And it avoids the ugly spectacle of a scandalous, deadbeat church.

Let us give as those who are glad to have a part in upholding the financial integrity of God's work.

Giving to the Next Generation

2 Chronicles 5:1

> *Thus all the work that Solomon made for the house of the Lord was finished: and Solomon brought in all the things that David his father had dedicated; and the silver, and the gold, and all the instruments, put he among the treasures of the house of God.*

EVEN THOUGH DAVID WAS a man after God's own heart, he was not permitted to build the temple. Instead, God appointed Solomon, David's son, the leader of the next generation, for that task.

But David did lay up many treasures and materials that were used in the construction of the temple. David left behind an offering for the next generation.

How many of us think in terms of "next generation" giving? How many believers actively plan and lay aside offerings for generations to come? How many Christians remember the church in their will, in their investments, in their obituary?

Many funeral notices invite friends and family to send a donation to a favorite charity in the name of the deceased in lieu of sending flowers. But instead of listing a secular charity, why not arrange to have donations sent to your local church in your name? It would be a wonderful way to give an offering to the next generation.

A man or woman after God's own heart certainly remembers to

give to God's work in the present generation, but they also delight in making an offering to the generation that will follow them in the gospel.

Let us give as those who have an eye for our own generation in the gospel, and the generation that will follow.

How Much Is Enough?

Acts 20:7

> *And upon the first day of the week, when the disciples came together to break bread, Paul preached unto them, ready to depart on the morrow; and continued his speech until midnight.*

ASSEMBLING TOGETHER ON THE first day of the week is a New Testament distinctive. It is a day for breaking bread, preaching, gathering in with other believers, and giving offerings.

The service mentioned in this verse seems long by modern, Western standards. It would not seem long in some other cultures.

Some have attempted to mine humor from the length of Paul's message described in our text, but the truth is that the record suggests that nobody departed early. In fact, even in the face of tragedy turned to victory, when a young man named Eutychus fell out of an upper window and appeared to be dead until Paul raised him up by the power of God, it seems that everyone stayed for the entire meeting.

The believers described in our text did not seem to feel inconvenienced or imposed upon because of the demands placed upon their time and whatever material supply they had furnished for the meeting. They gladly entered into the service and stayed until the victorious end.

Are we as tolerant, glad, and even enthusiastic about giving our time and material supply toward demanding circumstances in God's work in our own local church? Are we willing to make an offering of time or finances when there is a need in God's work? Have we signed on to stay until the glorious victory is won, or are we all too glad to take the side door out when circumstances require our diligence and faithfulness?

Let us give as those who have put no limitations on their resources or time in respect to God's work through the local church.

An "Around the Clock" Offering

Psalm 134:1–3

> *Behold, bless ye the Lord, all ye servants of the Lord, which by night stand in the house of the Lord. Lift up your hands in the sanctuary, and bless the Lord. The Lord that made heaven and earth bless thee out of Zion.*

OUR GOD NEVER SLUMBERS nor sleeps. Even in the deepest part of the night, servants of the Lord are to lift up their hands and bless the Lord.

The work of God is going on somewhere on the earth all the time. When it is night here, it is day somewhere else. His work never ceases. We sleep; He does not. There is always a work to be done, somewhere; always a need, day and night.

When we give our offerings to God's work, we not only give for the maintenance of a church building that may be open for only a few hours a week. We give to further the ministry of the gospel that goes on day and night—somewhere—all the time.

When is the proper time to give an offering? Anytime, day or night. There is no closed season.

Let us give as those who are ready to give at any hour of any day.

"Someday, When I've Got a Million Dollars!"

1 Corinthians 16:2

> *Upon the first day of the week let every one of you lay by him in store, as God hath prospered him, that there be no gatherings when I come.*

THIS VERSE HAS OFTEN BEEN used to show that we ought to bring our offerings to the Lord on Sundays. Although that is a good idea, it is not the only principle found in this verse. The apostle also talks about giving *as God has prospered us*, or giving in proportion to whatever amount the Lord has allowed us to manage as stewards or caretakers.

We need to give, realistically, all that we are able to give, all that it is within our power to give.

Some will say, "If I had a million dollars, I'd give it to the Lord's work." This is a noble intention, but it has nothing to do with our stewardship over what we actually do possess. The reality is that we are not responsible to God for the "million dollars" we might have someday, but we are responsible to God for the material and financial possessions we presently have!

The "someday scenario" must not be allowed to soothe our conscience when we are convicted of unfaithful giving, no matter how well intentioned we may be.

Let us give as those who are being faithful stewards of what they actually possess.

It Really Isn't Yours, You Know

Exodus 36:2

> *And Moses called Bezaleel and Aholiab, and every wise*
> *hearted man, in whose heart the Lord had put wisdom, even*
> *every one whose heart stirred him up to come unto the work*
> *to do it.*

WHAT A GIGANTIC OFFERING! The assembly of the materials for constructing the Old Testament tabernacle in the wilderness represents one of the most magnificent examples of stewardship in Bible history.

When the Israelites departed from Egypt during the Exodus, the Egyptians were more than happy to see them go and they pressed offerings of precious metals and stones into the hands of the departing Hebrews. Now these former slaves were rich, in a sense, and although they failed in other areas of their lives, they certainly did not fail in regard to their stewardship.

God did not give this wealth into the hands of these emancipated slaves so they could simply lavish themselves with a comfortable and opulent lifestyle. God had a much higher purpose. For it was out of this wealth that the offering for the construction of the tabernacle would be given. The lesson here is that the Israelites did not really own these things. They were stewards of them for the purpose and work of God.

Do we think of our possessions in this way? Maybe not. But we should realize that when we stand before God someday to give an account of our stewardship, He will not be very impressed with all of our toys. Do we, in our postmodern, computer driven, techno-proud, self-absorbed, "me" generation, really understand as much about our stewardship as these former slaves did?

Let us give as those who truly understand God's plan in entrusting His people with material possessions.

Catching Up with Simon Peter and Andrew

Matthew 4:20

And they straightway left their nets, and followed him.

"THEY" IN THIS VERSE ARE Simon Peter and Andrew. The "him" they followed is the Lord Jesus Christ. They immediately and completely responded to the Savior's call!

Do you think you have sacrificed much and responded quickly to the Lord's leading in your life? How do you measure up to these two men? They left *everything*—and they left *immediately*. There does not seem to have been any arguing, excuses, or faltering. They followed the Lord's instructions, no questions asked. Friends, family, future plans, business projections, all were left behind.

How do we measure up to this kind of faithfulness and stewardship? Have we really placed all of our time, our assets, energies, and desires at His feet for His disposal? Have we caught up with Simon Peter and Andrew?

Our present culture teaches us that we must live our own lives and perhaps carve out a little space for God, if it's convenient. The concept of stewardship demonstrated by Peter and Andrew is unthinkable by today's standards. But, should it be?

Do you have any nets that you're still trying to hold on to?

Let us give as those who have left their nets.

Offerings That Really Count for God

2 Chronicles 7:1

> *Now when Solomon had made an end of praying, the fire*
> *came down from heaven, and consumed the burnt offering*
> *and the sacrifices; and the glory of the Lord filled the house.*

WHAT A SPECTACULAR VERSE! What a sight it must have been, to see the fire of God come down from heaven and consume the offering and the sacrifices. If we had been there that day, we would have done just what the people of that day did. They bowed down with their faces to the pavement and worshiped. Nothing else would do in those circumstances.

The verse tells us that the offering of that day was *consumed*. The implication is that there was nothing left over. And so it is when God's fire falls upon an offering. It is used entirely. Nothing is wasted. In the Old Testament, when offerings were made with a fire kindled by men, the Mosaic Law allowed for the disposal of the leftovers. But not so with God's fire, because with God's fire there was nothing left over.

We may give an offering to man-made charities, but there is always a waste factor—overhead expenses and the percentage that never gets used for the original purpose. This problem is exposed often enough in news reports. But an offering given in God's way to God's work— through the local, New Testament Church—is not wasteful. As the offerings are used according to biblical instructions, the fire of God consumes it all for His work and the glory of the Lord fills His house.

Let us give as those who would direct their offerings away from wasteful, man-made fires and have them placed where God will wholly consume them.

Something Worth More Than Silver and Gold

Acts 3:6

> *Then Peter said, Silver and gold have I none; but such as I have give I thee: In the name of Jesus Christ of Nazareth rise up and walk.*

WE MIGHT CALL HIM A panhandler today—a beggar. Such a man asked Peter and John for some money outside the entrance to the temple. What better place to demonstrate the true riches of God in Christ Jesus?

There are two things about this verse that we should not miss.

First, there are always those in this world who have a genuine need of help and material assistance. We Christians need to guard against cynicism in a day when professional beggars are too often seen. There are still those who have genuine needs. Jesus said that these would always be with us. Peter responded to the beggar's need with what he had. He did not dismiss him as "probably just another crook."

Second, the servant of the Lord Jesus Christ has something better than silver and gold to give. This does not excuse us from charitable work in a material sense, but it does give us our priority for giving. We have something—some*one*—more valuable than silver or gold to give to the needy. Peter introduced this poor man to the power and person of the Lord Jesus Christ. That was the best offering he could have given him.

Peter declared that he did not have money to give. But even if he had, he would not have done the man any eternal good without introducing him to the Lord Jesus Christ.

Our offerings should not be looked upon as giving simply to quiet the voice of need. We should give through the local church in the name of the Lord Jesus Christ so that otherwise-doomed sinners may have a more important need met in their lives—the need for salvation, which can only be met in Him.

Let us give as those who have something more valuable than silver and gold to offer a dying world.

Is There Really a Priority for Our Giving?

Galatians 6:10

> *As we have therefore opportunity, let us do good unto all men, especially unto them who are of the household of faith.*

Do good to all men IS A maxim that most people would not dispute. Neither does the Bible dispute it. But in Scripture, there is a priority attached. Particular attention is to be given to helping those who are of the household of God. There is an order of priority here. Whatever we can do in our stewardship, we are to direct first of all to the ministry of those who are already part of the household of faith. Such a directive does not exclude anyone outside of the faith, but it does teach us where our first and finest efforts need to be made.

We are to do good to everyone as we have opportunity—doing the most good with what we have been given. We may not be able to do everything, but we can do something.

When the tithe and our offerings are given through the local church, we indeed give the proper priority to those of the household of faith.

Let us give as those who have extended their hands toward the household of faith first.

Filthy Rich and Miserable

James 5:1

> *Go to now, ye rich men, weep and howl for your miseries that shall come upon you.*

RICHES DO NOT MAKE A person miserable. But those who have placed their hopes for happiness and fulfillment in their riches will weep and howl at the end when they find out how hollow their comfort and reward is.

The believer understands that true riches are to be found in Christ Jesus the Lord. It is in a personal walk and fellowship with Him through His local church that real joy is realized here on earth.

The believer understands that we have not received riches, possessions, and assets solely for our personal happiness, but rather for use in serving our Lord Jesus Christ. Faithful stewardship and service is a means of genuine personal satisfaction, both now and in eternity.

Weeping and howling, or rejoicing and satisfaction evermore. Which would you choose? Which have you chosen? The difference can be seen in how we use the riches of this world.

Let us give as those who find joy in the correct use of riches for the honor and glory of Jesus Christ.

Biblical Giving Helps the Church Do Things the Right Way

Exodus 39:42–43

> *According to all that the Lord commanded Moses, so the children of Israel made all the work. And Moses did look upon all the work, and, behold, they had done it as the Lord had commanded, even so had they done it: and Moses blessed them.*

THE TABERNACLE OF THE Old Testament was now complete. All of the accompanying fixtures and garments were ready. Moses looked upon the finished work and declared it to be true to the standard that God had given him on the mount.

The successful completion of the work was made possible, in part, by the generous offerings the people had given. In fact, the people had given so much that it had been necessary to ask them to stop giving. What a marvelous testimony for the people of God.

How often today is the Lord's church hindered because of a spirit of giving that runs contrary to the example set by the congregation of Israel? Many Christians will gladly suffer the church to be turned into a secondhand discount clothing store or a cheap restaurant so that money can be raised for gospel work. But give sacrificially and faithfully? Not on your raffle ticket!

The true mission, nature, and focus of the church are often lost on the unsaved community because the church is forced to send mixed signals. Is it God's house, making the Good News of Jesus Christ available without charge? Or is it a religious fund-raising machine, grasping at any scheme to rake in a few dollars because of the hardness of its members?

Convenience giving and giving by fund-raising schemes makes the church look like something other than what Jesus intended it to be. Biblical giving helps the church do things the right way.

Let us give as those who realize that God intended for the giving of His people to be the source of financing for the local church.

Should You Be Ashamed of the Way You Use Your Money?

1 John 2:28–29

> *And now, little children, abide in him; that, when he shall appear, we may have confidence, and not be ashamed before him at his coming. If ye know that he is righteous, ye know that every one that doeth righteousness is born of him.*

RIGHTEOUS LIVING MEANS living right according to God's rules, not according to our feeling or whims. It means living each day in obedience to His words and heeding His written directions from the Scriptures.

Someday, when we stand before Him, we do not want to be ashamed because we did the wrong thing with our lives, or because we did not live according to His rules. Certainly, Christianity is not all about rules, but there would be no Christianity worth speaking about if we decided to ignore God's rules.

What about our giving to Christ's work through His local church? Will we one day stand ashamed before Him because we did not do the right thing, the righteous thing, with our offerings?

Will we one day discover, upon His accounting, that we spent more on entertainment, sports, and pleasurable things than we did in His service? Will we find ourselves ashamed? Think about it.

Is it possible we're spending more on the dog, the cat, or even the goldfish than we do in the service of our Lord Jesus Christ through His local church?

Let us give as those who will not be ashamed when He appears.

The Gospel Credit Card

Philemon 18

> *If he hath wronged thee, or oweth thee ought, put that on mine account.*

WHEN PAUL WROTE TO Philemon to plead on behalf of the former servant, Onesimus, who was now a Christian, there was some old business to be settled.

Before Onesimus became a Christian, he had perhaps been a little less than trustworthy. Perhaps he had run up some debts in the service of his master. There were some old bills to be paid.

Paul could have done the same thing that many Christians do today. He could have left Onesimus to face the music. After all, he made his bed, let him lie in it. But this was not Paul's way. Nor should it be ours.

Paul wanted Philemon to receive Onesimus, not as a servant but as a beloved brother. Paul says, "If he hath wronged thee, or oweth thee ought, put that on mine account." This is much like the Good Samaritan, whom Jesus Christ spoke of in His parable, who gave carte blanche to the innkeeper.

If credit card machines had existed in Paul's day, he might have said, "I've swiped my card, Philemon, now you fill in the amount."

Such an attitude is not exclusive to the apostles and characters in parables. It ought also to reflect our attitude toward God and His work every day. Are we ready to give what is needed, or are we measuring and weighing every gift lest we overdo our generosity?

Paul's magnificent offer is an example that should motivate our giving.

Let us give as those who would dare to give God a blank check for the sake of the gospel.

The Only Offering That Will Purchase Favor with God

Hebrews 10:6

> *In burnt offerings and sacrifices for sin thou hast had no pleasure.*

THERE IS ONLY ONE OFFERING that could purchase God's favor on our behalf—the offering of our Lord Jesus Christ on Calvary's cross.

All the animal offerings and sacrifices that happened before the coming of Christ could not purchase God's favor. Those offerings were a picture, a representation, of Christ's eventual offering at Calvary, but God could take no lasting pleasure in them.

Our salvation is neither found nor sustained in the offering plate. Believers do not give to gain favor with God. We give because we have *already* gained favor with God through faith in the once-and-for-all offering of our Lord Jesus Christ on the cross. The truth here is simple but overwhelmingly profound.

Understanding the significance of Christ's offering for our sins does not reduce the importance of our material offerings. But it should lead us to give in the full assurance and joy of a saving faith that desires to serve God.

Let us give as those who have already had their favor with God purchased through the offering of the Lord Jesus Christ on Calvary.

When the Offering Is Reduced to a Mere Business Transaction

John 2:15–16

> *And when he had made a scourge of small cords, he drove them all out of the temple, and the sheep, and the oxen; and poured out the changers' money, and overthrew the tables; and said unto them that sold doves, Take these things hence; make not my Father's house an house of merchandise.*

WHAT COULD BE MORE REPUGNANT to Jesus than to see the temple turned into a lucrative business market? In the guise of furnishing necessary supplies for the required temple offerings, some were making quite a handsome profit for themselves. The heavenly Father's house— the intended house of prayer— had become a house of merchandise.

What happens when the love, service, and worship of God is suddenly reduced to a common business transaction? This kind of a situation isn't as farfetched in our day as we might think.

Do we give our offerings out of love and obedience to our Lord Jesus Christ? Or have we reduced the offering to nothing more than a business transaction in our mind? We may reason that the offering is a necessary nuisance so that the church can pay its bills. But such thinking is grievous and repulsive to our Lord.

We must never allow the offering to be reduced to nothing more than a piece of business. It must always be a loving, devotional, passionate act of worship, freely and generously given.

Let us give as those who love God with a holy passion, not as those who are simply carrying out a business transaction.

Choose: Rich and Rebellious, or Poor and Obedient?

Proverbs 28:6

> *Better is the poor that walketh in his uprightness, than he that is perverse in his ways, though he be rich.*

HERE IS ONE OF THOSE TRUTHS OF Scripture that must be set before us only because it is so obvious and purely simple that we might overlook it: It is better to be poor and right with God than to be rich and sinful. Although most of us understand that we ought to agree with this sentiment, when given a choice, the uncomfortable truth is that the riches and sin seem to win out more often.

Most people who do not give an offering to the Lord's work as they should are governed by the false notion that whatever they give will diminish their resources and leave them that much poorer. Most people who give as they should have discovered that this really is a false notion. It just isn't true.

The writer of the proverb is saying, in part, that even if this false notion were true, it would still be better to give to God as we should and be counted as poor than to have wealth at the expense of being sinful by disobeying God.

If we give according to the principles of Scripture, and if we give with a heart that is fixed in a right relationship with God, we will never be the poorer. We may not have everything we desire in life, but we will have everything we need.

Does such a way of thinking disturb you? If it does, perhaps a worldly way of reasoning has crept into your thought processes. Come, let us reason together with the penman of Holy Writ. We need not be poor, but it is better that we should be poor than disobey God.

Let us give as those who need not be poor, but who would be willing to be made poor in the service of the King of kings.

A Good Investment

Philippians 2:16

> *Holding forth the word of life; that I may rejoice in the day of Christ, that I have not run in vain, neither laboured in vain.*

EVERY GENUINE BELIEVER SHOULD want to hold forth the word of life, to make the gospel of our Lord Jesus Christ available to all without charge. Such work is not merely a noble sentiment; it is a divine urging.

The apostle is not saying here that he hopes he has not labored in vain; he is saying that because he has invested in holding forth the word of life, he is certain that he has not labored in vain! He declares that holding forth the word of life has been a good investment of his life, his time, his talents, and his treasures.

For Christians to do anything less than invest their time, talents, and treasures in holding forth the word of life would be to labor in vain, wasting precious time and resources. We can make no better investment on this planet than to give to God's work through His local church.

Let us give to the local church as those who are serious about making a good investment for the Lord Jesus Christ.

Giving: A Whim or a Work of Grace?

Matthew 9:9

> *And as Jesus passed forth from thence, he saw a man, named Matthew, sitting at the receipt of custom: and he saith unto him, Follow me. And he arose, and followed him.*

IN THE SPAN OF ONE VERSE, Matthew the hated tax collector becomes Matthew the beloved disciple and apostle.

We may not enjoy being taxed by our local and federal governments, but we understand the system and take it seriously. Honest believers are careful to meet their tax obligations.

Why is it, then, that so many struggle with the idea that there might be a form of taxation established by the government of our heavenly Father? Who said that we should never feel a financial obligation to the government of the kingdom of God? Who said that any giving to the church must be painless? Who said that the church should be financed by fund-raising schemes? Who said that Christians should never make sacrificial gifts?

Is Jesus really the Governor of our soul? If so, it should not seem strange that He would ask a tax upon our time, our talents, and our treasures, whatever they may be.

Our giving is not to be predicated upon our personal whim. Instead, it is to be a work of grace in our hearts that matures and develops as we come into closer fellowship with the Governor of our soul. We gladly submit to the taxation of His kingdom.

Let us give as those who are happy to enter into the taxation system of the kingdom of our Lord Jesus Christ.

"I'm Doing an Awful Lot for God!"

Mark 10:28

Then Peter began to say unto him, Lo, we have left all, and have followed thee.

HERE IS YET ANOTHER EXAMPLE of why Peter is so lovable to many Christians. He reflects the humanity and shortcomings that we often see in ourselves as we stumble along trying our best to serve the Savior.

Peter must have been feeling a little bit sorry for himself. Perhaps he was thinking of the lucrative possibilities of commercial life that he had left behind. Perhaps he was beginning to see that in following Jesus he was probably never going to be a rich man. Whatever his reasoning, he blurts out, "Look here, Lord, we have left everything to follow after you." Self-pity and self-righteousness rolled up into one neat little package.

Our Lord Jesus Christ is quick to set Peter, and us, straight on this topic. In the next three verses following Peter's outburst, Jesus shows Peter how much he has gained and by eternal reckoning how he has actually lost nothing.

The "Peter Syndrome" is very easy to embrace—and it is contagious! Let's be careful to keep our ears tuned to the words of Jesus here and not the words of Peter. It is Jesus who has done an awful lot for *us*!

Let us give as those who realize that they have not given too much, whereas Jesus has given everything.

Does God Still Want Presents?

Psalm 76:11

> *Vow, and pay unto the Lord your God: let all that be round about him bring presents unto him that ought to be feared.*

THIS OLD TESTAMENT VERSE sets three important concepts before us, even though we are New Testament believers:

- The concept of the vow—making a commitment to God and sticking to it. We live in a sad time when almost everyone is willing to make financial vows for everything except the gospel, and to anyone except God.
- The concept of bringing presents to the Lord. Our "me" generation mind-set suggests to us that perhaps God is the one who should be bringing presents to us. Prosperity theology has done much to feed this reverse way of thinking.
- The concept of fearing God. This concept has nothing to do with living in stark terror of some omnipotent being; it has everything to do with being concerned about God's approval of us. Does He approve of our lives, of our gifts to Him?

Making vows to God, bringing Him presents, and fearing Him in a biblical way are all part of our worship. These are durable biblical concepts of giving that have not passed their "sell-by" date. God wants us to vow to Him, to fear Him, and to bring Him presents.

Let us give as those who understand and enjoy the durable concepts of biblical giving.

The Show-off at the Offering Plate

Matthew 6:1

> *Take heed that ye do not your alms before men, to be seen of them: otherwise ye have no reward of your Father which is in heaven.*

JESUS IS NOT SPEAKING HERE about how *much* we give, but rather *how* we give.

If we are giving with the thought of impressing others, we might actually succeed. Others may stand in awe and exclaim that we are doing wonderful things for the Lord. But if these accolades occur with our consent and complicity, then we will have received our full reward in whatever praise or reputation we have gained. But God has no reward for us in heaven after that.

An offering given out of obedience to God, out of love and fear of Him, out of a generous spirit toward the local church, comes much closer to divine notice.

It is more important that we impress God with our motives for giving than that we impress those around us with the actions of our giving.

Let us give as much and as often as we should for the approval of God, not others.

Is a Painless Offering a Good Thing?

2 Samuel 24:24

And the king said unto Araunah, Nay; but I will surely buy it of thee at a price: neither will I offer burnt offerings unto the Lord my God of that which doth cost me nothing. So David bought the threshingfloor and the oxen for fifty shekels of silver.

NO WONDER DAVID IS DESCRIBED as a man after God's own heart! He would not offer to God something that cost him nothing! David not only refused to give a painless offering, he seemed to despise the very idea.

How contrary is our thinking to that of David in the matter of giving an offering to the Lord?

The attitude of our current generation toward giving to the local church seems to be, "Let's only give what is painless, and what will never be missed anyway." How strange this kind of thinking would be to a man like David.

Pastors and other church leaders are often muzzled on the topic of giving, because of a subtle yet hostile attitude that exists among the members, who act as if they should never be urged to make any kind of sacrificial gift.

Nobody wants to make the offering a painful thing, but we must be wary of the notion that it should always be painless.

Let us give with the heart of David, refusing the idea of the painless offering.

Choosing the Right Bank

2 Peter 3:11

> *Seeing then that all these things shall be dissolved, what manner of persons ought ye to be in all holy conversation and godliness?*

WHAT A PROFOUND THOUGHT! Everything we can see and touch, everything that is a point of reference or that has furnished us with our life experiences, is to be dissolved. They will one day pass from existence.

This is not intended to be a morbid or depressing thought. It is intended as a warning, a caution toward preparation. Everything that looks so permanent is really very temporary and will be removed within the will and timing of God.

If all of this is true—and we believe it is—we should ask ourselves, as honest Christians: "In which reality am I investing my time, talents, and treasures? In this temporary reality, or in the eternal reality to come? Which do I really believe is most important?"

If we accept the truth revealed in the Bible that this temporary reality will pass from existence, then we will want to invest in the bank of eternity. Regular deposits can be made in this eternal bank. Branch offices are located everywhere. They are called the local church.

Let us give as those who realize that the divine bankruptcy notice has already been served on the banks and financial institutions of this temporary reality.

Is God First or Last?

Exodus 22:29–30

> *Thou shalt not delay to offer the first of thy ripe fruits, and of thy liquors: the firstborn of thy sons shalt thou give unto me. Likewise shalt thou do with thine oxen, and with thy sheep: seven days it shall be with his dam; on the eight day thou shalt give it me.*

THE CEREMONIAL LAW OF THE Old Testament may not be binding on New Testament believers, but the old canon is a wonderful place to observe the mind of God. His intentions and ways of thinking are so clearly set before us there.

One thing we learn from this and other Old Testament verses is that God wants the first and the best in our offerings. He isn't interested in receiving our leftovers, our castoffs, and things we don't want. In a manner of speaking, he doesn't want us to throw Him a bone as if He were an old dog.

When we plan our giving, do we give God the first and the best? Or do we convince ourselves that we'll do better in our giving "someday" when our finances are in better shape?

Which end of the budget does God occupy? The bottom end, where we graciously throw Him a few leftover scraps, if there are any? Or, does He occupy the top end of our budget, where we pay Him first and give Him the best we can?

Where is God in your budget? First or last?

Let us give as those who would not resign God to last place in the family budget.

Your Giving Says Something About You

Luke 3:8

> *Bring forth therefore fruits worthy of repentance, and begin not to say within yourselves, We have Abraham to our father: for I say unto you, That God is able of these stones to raise up children unto Abraham.*

JOHN THE BAPTIST DID NOT worry about being politically correct. He said the things that had to be said. Such is the character of a good prophet.

Although multitudes had attended his preaching and baptism services, it seems clear that John realized there were some who understood very little, if anything, about his baptism.

In this verse, John calls for the evidence of repentance from any who would be baptized. He was interested in a fit evidence of their conversion, not just in dipping them in the river.

According to the apostle Paul, giving is one of the graces of Christianity that is evident in a believer. It is one of the proofs that we are saved.

Ask yourself these questions: Does my giving provide clear evidence that I have really been saved? Do I give gladly, joyfully, and as generously as possible, or do I merely tolerate the offering as some kind of unavoidable annoyance?

Sporadic giving, stingy giving, grudging giving, or the absence of giving and the loads of excuses that go with it—are these really the clear evidence of a repentant soul that is serving God cheerfully?

Let us give as those who would give evidence of their priorities by their giving.

Scripture Index